carnivores

Heather C. Hudak

WEIGL PUBLISHERS INC.

Published by Weigl Publishers Inc.
350 5th Avenue, Suite 3304, PMB 6G
New York, NY 10118-0069 USA
Web site: www.weigl.com

Library of Congress Cataloging-in-Publication Data

Hudak, Heather C., 1975-
  Carnivores / Heather C. Hudak.
      p. cm. -- (Nature's food chain)
  Includes index.
  ISBN 1-59036-238-1 (lib. bdg. : alk. paper) 1-59036-262-4 (pbk.)
  1. Carnivora--Juvenile literature. I. Title. II. Series.
  QL737.C2H83 2004
  599.74--dc22

                                    2004012600

Printed in the United States of America
1 2 3 4 5 6 7 8 9 0   08 07 06 05 04

Project Coordinator Janice L. Redlin **Design and Layout** Bryan Pezzi
Copy Editor Tina Schwartzenberger **Photo Research** Andrea Harvey

Photograph Credits
Every reasonable effort has been made to trace ownership and to obtain permission to reprint copyright material. The publishers would be pleased to have any errors or omissions brought to their attention so that they may be corrected in subsequent printings.

Cover: cougar (**Photos.com**); **Phillip Colla:** page 15T; **CORBIS/MAGMA:** pages 8L (Enzo & Paolo Ragazzini), 8R (Enzo & Paolo Ragazzini), 15M (Frank Lane Picture Agency); **Corel Corporation:** pages 3, 5R, 7B, 20TL, 20ML, 20BL, 20BM, 20BR; **Heather C. Hudak:** page 9T; **Martha Jones:** page 11B; **Photos.com:** pages 1, 4, 5T, 5L, 5M, 5B, 6, 7T, 9B, 10, 12, 13T, 14T, 14B, 15B, 18, 19T, 19B, 20TM, 20TR, 20MM, 20MR, 22; **Visuals Unlimited:** pages 11T (Joe McDonald), 13B (Dr. Gary Gaugler).

On the Cover: Cougars are solitary animals that feed primarily on deer.

All of the Internet URLs given in the book were valid at the time of publication. However, due to the dynamic nature of the Internet, some addresses may have changed, or sites may have ceased to exist since publication. While the author and publisher regret any inconvenience this may cause readers, no responsibility for any such changes can be accepted by either the author or the publisher.

Contents

Nature's Food Chain

All living things need food to survive. Food provides the energy that plants and animals need to grow and thrive. Plants and animals do not rely on the same types of food to live. Plants make their own food. They use energy from the Sun and water from the soil. Some animals eat plants. Others eat animals that have already eaten plants. In this way, living things rely on each other and form a food chain.

A food chain is made up of **producers** and **consumers**. Plants are the only producers in the food chain. This is because they make energy. This energy can be used by the rest of the living things on Earth. The other living things are called consumers. There are four different types of consumers in a food chain. They are herbivores, carnivores, omnivores, and decomposers. All of the world's animals belong to one of these consumer groups. The second level of consumers in the food chain is called carnivores.

Hawks use their razor sharp claws to kill prey, such as mice, snakes, and other birds.

Did you know?

If an animal's food source disappears, other animals will suffer and possibly die.

Food Chain Connections

The Sun

Decomposer (consumer)

Omnivore (consumer)

CARNIVORE (CONSUMER)

Herbivore (consumer)

Plant (producer)

5

What is a Carnivore?

Carnivore means "meat eater." It is a Latin word. The term carnivore describes animals in the food chain that eat the flesh of other animals. Carnivores get their energy from eating the meat of other living things. Most carnivores eat herbivores. Herbivores are plant-eating animals. Some carnivores eat omnivores. Omnivores are animals that eat both plants and meat. Many carnivores hunt and kill their own **prey**. Some carnivores eat dead animals. Cheetahs, crocodiles, great white sharks, weasels, and wolves are all examples of carnivores. Some insects and birds are also carnivores.

Crocodiles use their tails to move fish closer together so they are easier to eat.

Carnivores hunt their food. They must eat a large number of **calories** so they have enough energy to hunt. Some carnivores, such as wolves and some dolphins, hunt as a group. It is easier for a group to catch large prey. The animals in the group share the catch. Other carnivores, such as lynx, wait for prey to come near. Then they pounce on the prey. This is called lie-and-wait hunting. Some carnivores that lie and wait for prey are camouflaged. This means they blend into their environment. Other carnivores attract prey to them. For example, the viperfish has 350 tiny lights inside its mouth. These lights act as a lure, or bait. Once prey are near, the viperfish uses its long sharp teeth to grab its food.

Occasionally, a wolf will hunt on its own. It can catch smaller animals, such as beavers, birds, rabbits, and raccoons.

Did you know?

The polar bear is the largest land carnivore. Most polar bears weigh more than 700 pounds (318 kilograms).

Built for Meat Eating

All carnivores have features that are **adapted** to their diets. Many carnivores have special body parts that help them chew and **digest** meat.

Among the most important body features for all carnivores are the teeth. Carnivore teeth are designed for eating meat. Carnivores have short, pointed **incisors** for nipping and biting. They have sharp **canine** teeth for stabbing and holding prey. Carnivores have **premolar** teeth. These teeth are used for cutting and slicing flesh. Carnivores have **molars** for grinding and crushing bones.

Examine the photos of a carnivore's teeth and a herbivore's teeth. What differences do you see?

Comparing Animal Jaws

Carnivore jaw (crocodile)

Herbivore jaw (kangaroo)

Most carnivores have very keen senses. Senses help them locate their prey. Felines, or cats, can see very well. During the day, they see about the same quality as humans. At night, a part of a cat's eye opens wide to let more light shine through. This allows cats to see well in the dark. Felines can hear well, too. A feline can turn its ears to hear even the quietest sounds. This feature helps them know the type and size of prey in their environment.

Most cats are active at night. They use their excellent night vision to hunt and capture their prey in the dark.

Some carnivores have a very keen sense of smell. Hyenas and dingoes use their sense of smell to track prey.

Did you know?

The jaws of many carnivores move up and down. This helps them tear and bite meat.

Ravenous Reptiles

Many different kinds of reptiles are carnivores. Reptiles eat eggs, insects, and small **vertebrates**, such as **amphibians**, birds, fish, **rodents**, and other reptiles. Carnivorous reptiles catch prey in many ways. Most reptiles, such as alligators and snakes, have sharp teeth. Some reptiles have long claws. Komodo dragons use their claws to grab and rip their prey. This allows them to eat large animals such as goats, monkeys, and wild pigs.

The komodo dragon has at least four types of deadly bacteria in its saliva. When a komodo dragon bites its prey, the bacteria can kill the victim within a week.

Boa constrictors do not have claws. Instead, the boa wraps its body tightly around the prey. After some time, the prey can no longer breathe. When the prey dies, the boa swallows the entire animal headfirst. Boas can stretch their jaws wide open to swallow animals much larger than their heads.

The boa constrictor feeds primarily on birds, lizards, small mammals, and rodents.

Another type of carnivorous reptile is the crocodile. This large animal has thirty to forty teeth on each jaw. These teeth fit together when the crocodile closes its mouth. Crocodiles swim underwater with just their nostrils and eyes above the surface. They sneak up on their prey. Then they drag the animal underwater and hold it until it drowns. Crocodiles can crush small animals by snapping their mouths closed on the animal.

Did you know?

Most reptiles have a Jacobson's organ in their mouth. This organ helps reptiles taste and smell. They use the Jacobson's organ to hunt prey, find mates, and know what is in their surroundings.

Creepy Crawlies

There are more than 40,000 **species** of spiders. All spiders are carnivorous. They eat insects, other spiders, and small vertebrates, such as birds and frogs. There are two types of spiders. Ground spiders hunt their prey. Web spiders spin webs to catch prey. Most spiders use venom, or poison, to kill or **paralyze** their prey before eating it.

A web spider's body produces an oil that prevents it from getting stuck to its own web.

Tarantulas are large, hairy spiders. Most tarantulas live in warm, tropical regions. They eat insects and other small animals. Tarantulas do not spin webs. They use speed and strength to sneak up on their prey. Then they pounce on the prey and bite it with their fangs. Unlike other carnivores, tarantulas do not have teeth for chewing. They can only drink their food. Tarantulas inject their prey with digestive juices. These juices turn the prey's insides into liquid. The tarantula sucks this liquid and leaves the prey's body behind.

Tarantulas have small hairs on their belly that they rub on their predators. This distracts the predators so the tarantula can escape.

Did you know?

Spiders stab their prey with long, pointed teeth called fangs. The fangs are located on the front of their mouth. Poison is released from the tip of the fang into the prey.

Carnivore Closeup

There are many different kinds of carnivores. They come in all shapes and sizes. Some of the world's largest and smallest animals are carnivores. Carnivores can be found throughout the world. Some carnivores live in water. Many live on land.

cheetah

- fastest land animal
- lives in Africa
- reaches speeds of 70 miles per hour (113 kilometers per hour)
- hunts during the day
- can live without water for long periods of time; cheetahs gather much of the water they need from the body fluids of their prey
- eats gazelles, hares, and impalas

Swift Fox

- smallest canine, or dog, in North America
- grows about 12 inches (30 centimeters) high
- lives in open spaces in North America
- reaches speeds of 25 miles per hour (40 kph)
- eats amphibians, birds, small mammals, and reptiles

Blue Whale

- largest animal on Earth; grows to more than 80 feet (24 meters) long

- travels from tropical ocean waters in the winter to **pack ice** in the summer

- uses **baleens** to filter prey from water

- lunges open-mouthed into schools of fish, krill, or plankton

- smallest mammal carnivore, about 4 to 10 inches (10–25 cm) long

- lives on farmland, stone walls, and in wooded areas

- can kill animals up to five times its size

- uses its claws and sharp teeth to catch prey

- eats small birds, mice, moles, rabbits, and rats

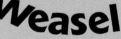

Least Weasel

Peregrine Falcon

- fastest bird

- reaches speeds between 180 and 200 miles per hour (290 and 322 kph)

- hunts by snatching prey in flight using its sharp talons, or claws

- uses a sharp, toothlike point on its beak to tear apart prey

- eats frogs, insects, rodents, and small birds, such as ducks, pigeons, and seabirds

Carnivore Habitats

All carnivores require special living conditions in order to thrive. The place where an animal lives is called its habitat. Earth has many different habitats. A carnivore's habitat can be as big as a desert or a forest. It can also be as small as a tree branch or a pond. Each carnivore must live where it can get the food it needs to survive. For example, stellar sea lions eat a variety of fish, such as flounder, herring, and pollock. They would not live long on grasslands.

Some of the world's largest habitats include deserts, grasslands, temperate forests, tropical rain forests, and tundra. Look at the map to see which types of carnivores live in each of these habitats. Can you think of other carnivores to add to each of these habitats?

Carnivores in the tundra: arctic foxes, polar bears, wolves

Carnivores in tropical rain forests: anacondas, jaguars, piranhas

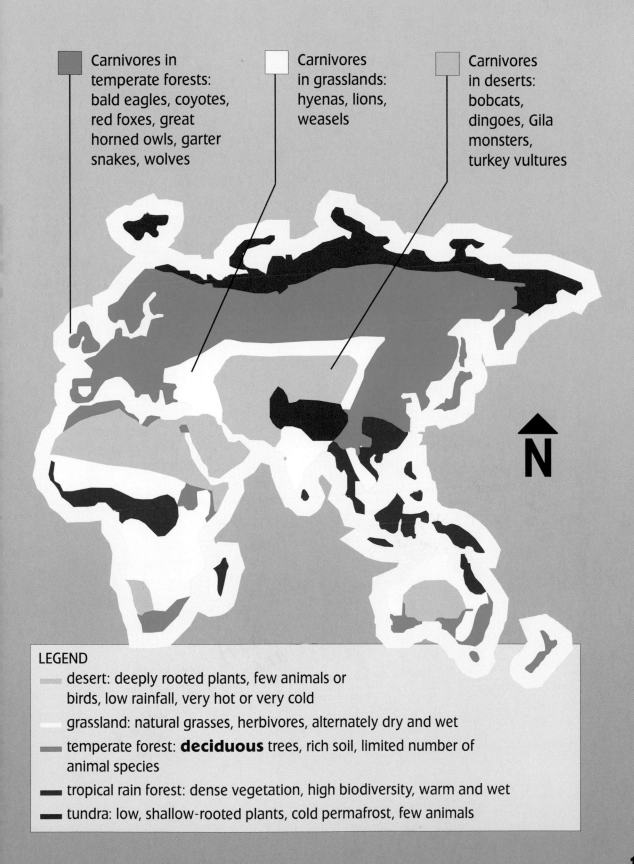

Carnivores in temperate forests: bald eagles, coyotes, red foxes, great horned owls, garter snakes, wolves

Carnivores in grasslands: hyenas, lions, weasels

Carnivores in deserts: bobcats, dingoes, Gila monsters, turkey vultures

N

LEGEND

desert: deeply rooted plants, few animals or birds, low rainfall, very hot or very cold

grassland: natural grasses, herbivores, alternately dry and wet

temperate forest: **deciduous** trees, rich soil, limited number of animal species

tropical rain forest: dense vegetation, high biodiversity, warm and wet

tundra: low, shallow-rooted plants, cold permafrost, few animals

Carnivores at Risk

Plants and animals rely on each other in order to survive. For example, carnivores eat herbivores that live in a region. Sometimes the carnivore moves to a new region or becomes **extinct**. If this happens, the herbivore population grows. The herbivores overeat the plants in the region. Over time, there will not be enough plant materials for the herbivores to eat. Another example is sea otters that eat sea urchins. Without sea otters, sea urchins overeat the kelp or seaweed in the region. This means other plants and animals, such as fish, and seabird **fauna**, cannot thrive. If there were no sea otters, kelp would die. If there were no kelp, fish and seabirds would die.

Sea otters swim on their backs, using their bellies to balance and carry food.

When a carnivore's habitat is destroyed and food is no longer available, that carnivore becomes **endangered**. Every day, carnivores, from insects to mammals, become endangered or extinct. An endangered carnivore puts herbivores and plants

at risk, too. In most cases, humans cause the world's plants and animals to become endangered. When people clear land to build communities or grow crops, many plants and animals lose their homes and their food supplies. Some environmental groups work to preserve the world's natural habitats.

Clearing land to build new communities causes carnivores, such as wolves and crocodiles, to live closer to humans.

Did you know?

The snow leopard is endangered. It lives at altitudes higher than 19,000 feet (6,000 m). Its solitary nature and remote habitat make it difficult for people and scientists to see and study.

Making a Food Chain

Plants and animals are linked together through food chains. In this way, all living things depend on one another for survival. Each one of the carnivores in these pictures is part of a unique food chain. Look closely at these carnivores. In what type of food chain do these animals belong? What does the animal eat? What animals eat it?

cougar

dolphin

spider

peregrine falcon

sea otter

tiger

wolf

crocodile

polar bear

Once you have examined all of the pictured animals, pick one and learn more about it. Using the Internet and your school library, find information about the animal's diet. Explore which animals the carnivore might eat. Draw a food chain that shows what you learned. If the carnivore you chose belongs to more than one food chain, create more than one. Write an explanation about why the carnivore does or does not belong to more than one food chain.

Do you have any pets that are carnivores? Do you know anyone who has a pet carnivore? If so, write something about what the carnivore eats. What special features does its body have that assists it in eating?

One example of a food chain starts with a plant (producer). Large animals, such as giraffes (herbivores), live on plants. Giraffes are eaten by consumers. Energy is transferred from one living thing to another in a food chain.

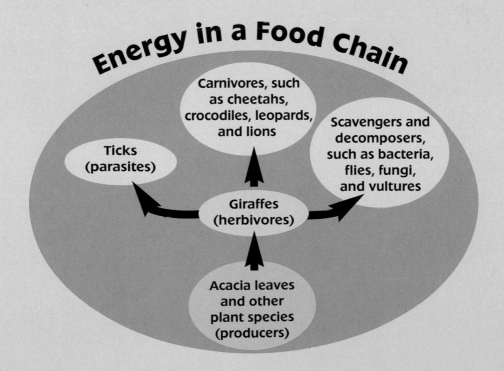

Energy in a Food Chain

Ticks (parasites)

Carnivores, such as cheetahs, crocodiles, leopards, and lions

Scavengers and decomposers, such as bacteria, flies, fungi, and vultures

Giraffes (herbivores)

Acacia leaves and other plant species (producers)

Quiz

Based on what you have just read, try to answer the following questions correctly.

1. What does the word carnivore mean?

2. What is the largest carnivore on Earth?

3. How many teeth do crocodiles have?

4. What does a viperfish have inside its mouth that acts as a lure?

5. What is the name of an endangered cat species?

6. How do tarantulas eat their food?

7. What do sea otters eat?

8. How do hyenas and dingoes hunt prey?

Answers: 1. Meat eater **2.** The blue whale **3.** 30 to 40 **4.** 350 tiny lights **5.** The snow leopard **6.** They turn their prey into liquid and suck the liquid through their mouth **7.** Sea urchins **8.** With their sense of smell

Further Research

There are many more interesting facts to learn about the world's carnivores. If you are interested in learning more, here are some places to start your research.

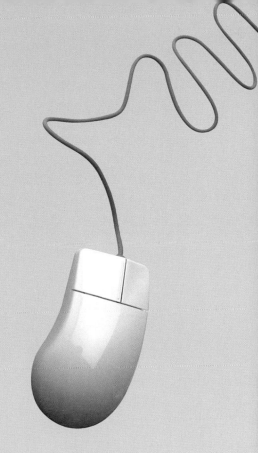

Web Sites

To learn more fascinating facts about carnivores, visit:

www.cptigers.org

To learn more about protecting carnivores, visit:

www.carnivoreconservation.org

For information about large carnivores in Europe, visit:

www.large-carnivores-lcie.org

Books

Swan, Erin Pembrey. *Land Predators Around the World*. New York: Franklin Watts, Incorporated, 2001.

Woods, Samuel G. *Sorting Out Mammals: Everything You Want to Know About Marsupials, Carnivores, Herbivores, and More!* Woodbridge, CT: Blackbirch Marketing, 1999.

Glossary

adapted: adjusted to make suitable

amphibians: cold-blooded animals with smooth skin that spend part of their life on land and part in water

baleens: horny material on the upper jaw that acts as a filter

calories: units that measure the amount of energy a food produces when taken into the body

canine: pointed tooth located between the front and back teeth

consumers: animals that feed on plants or other animals

deciduous: type of tree with leaves that fall off each year

digest: to break down materials that can be used by the body

endangered: at risk of no longer living any place on Earth

extinct: no longer living any place on Earth

fauna: all the animal life in a particular region

incisors: front teeth used for cutting and gnawing

molars: large teeth used for grinding food

pack ice: a solid mass of floating ice covering a wide area, especially in polar regions

paralyze: to take away the ability to move

premolar: teeth located before the molars

prey: animals that are hunted by other animals for food

producers: living things, such as plants, that produce their own food

rodents: animals that have a pair of big front teeth used for gnawing

species: a group of the same kind of living thing; members can breed together

vertebrates: animals that have a backbone

Index